By Process of Illumination

∞

Poems by Peter Craig

Cover photo by Lisa Pelonzi

Note: the author's full name is Peter William Craig – no relation to American novelist and screenwriter Peter Craig, who is known for works such as *The Martini Shot* and *Blood Father*.

By Process of Illumination / Peter W. Craig

ISBN: 9798601415064

Subjects: Poetry, Spirituality

First edition 2020.

*For those who may still be in darkness,
but haven't given up.*

Acknowledgments

I wish to sincerely thank my siblings and sisters in law. Without their support it is possible that I might not even be here today. There are too many people to name here who gave kind and compassionate support to my wife. Dear friends from my church were also especially kind and supportive for me.

Although I occasionally wrote poetry for a very long time, it was Dr. Michael Guidi who suggested that I resume. Thank you to local poetry and open mic meetings, which gave me an audience and suggested improvements to some of these poems. Thank you also to photographer and friend Lisa Pelonzi for the beautiful cover photo and head shot. For more of her stunning photos of sunrises and newborns, please visit lisapelonzi.com.

Inspiration requires no human messenger, but there have been many teachers, books, and practices that gradually opened me to receive it. I'm grateful for all of them. While writing these poems it was Mooji whose guidance was the most direct and helpful.

Table of Contents

Overture

The path from grief to serenity

Learning from Loss

Did you ever lose someone so essential
that it undermines you?
When the tears finally flow,
it's a relief
from the shock and denial.

The present, so unacceptable.
Food, drinking, drugs, sleep,
offer the numbness
that postpones the inevitable:
your disagreement with reality.

A fog descends on the path forward.
Linger here in purgatory
if you must.

When the fog begins to clear,
thoughts of replacing them will spring up.
Smile upon them and let them go,
knowing they are spoiled by your neediness.

Fear will also rear its head.
One big loss
questions all that you still have.
Relax your grip on them.
Nothing belongs to you.

Now open your eyes wider,
look inside and see why it hurts.
You invested so much of yourself in them
that you feel diminished.
It's tempting to compensate
by building yourself up

and holding your own,
but it closes your heart.

So be diminished!
Create empty space inside.
Open the doors.
Allow life to come in,
and to go out.

And finally,
let go of your self.
It's really just an idea in your head.
I am a certain kind of person,
determined by the past,
determined to create the future.
Dropping this
you enter the river of life,
and are troubled no more.

≠

Part I: In Darkness

The unthinkable happens.
There is darkness.
A fog descends.
Life asks:
Who are you now?

Still Here

Torn and tattered
Discombobulated
Still breathing, still living

Story is broken
Future is scary
Still breathing, still living

Flooded with grief
Burning my heart
Still breathing, still living

The vast unknown
Empties me out
Still breathing, still living, still here

≠

The Burning

A thought rings out
Sparks fly from it
A sudden burning in my chest
Sound the alarm
Stop this scoundrel
Redirect and distract
The thought is put out
Still the burning lingers
In my chest
Finally extinguished by tears

There Are Moments

There are moments when the light comes through
There are clouds of dreaded future
There are whole meals of bittersweet grieving
There are cleansing showers of tears
There are sudden gasps as the future disappears
There are rants that stomp through my mind
There are tenuous new beginnings
There are sleepless hours of futility
There are hollow social pleasantries
There are vulnerable openings

Blown Away

Battered
by a troubled mind.
Gale force nocks me to my knees.
Who am I that can be pushed around
by thought and emotion?
The wind moves only what resists.
Unseen, it appears by proxy
through those that are moved.

This storm
of mind and heart
whips me with dust
'till all is black.
When the dust settles
and the sky is clear,
I see where I have been.

Clinging to shelter
from my dark imaginings.
Feeding them denial.
Refusing to change,
when change has already happened.
This is my resistance.
This is why
I am blown away.

≠

The Unmanageable Mind

It's a scattered world
whipped into a frenzy
by life's urgency.

No one can take it all in.
Boundaries protect us
from incomprehension.
They expand and contract
like the breath.

Sometimes they shrink
to nearly zero.
All is unacceptable.

The unmanageable mind
has behind it a presence
calling for attention.

But a thousand eruptions of thought
steal attention away.
The call is long ignored.

Am I lost or am I here?
Can I hear through my mind?
Eventually, there must be silence.

Can I Help You?

Call me if you need anything
I need no things
I need a peaceful presence

If I can help just let me know
No one can help
But you can be a witness

I'm sorry for your loss
Have I also lost you?
Or are you here with me?

You're doing so well
The doing is the easy part
It's when I sit alone...

Call me anytime
In my weakness I don't want to
In my strength I don't need to

The Heartwood

Intricate patterns of tangled thoughts.
The fabric of life,
finely tailored here,
and threadbare there

Wrapped in layers I venture out.
Peering at outer appearance.
Imagining inner structure.
How rare the glimpse at what lies within
unless we are broken open.
Tender vulnerability
then shares what needs repair.

Searching urgently
for someone to mend me.
Peeling off onion skins.
Casting off layers beyond repair.

Stripped to the core.
What remains is a seed.
Even that must be split
to allow a new sprout.

Falling on good soil,
years of growth rings
restore protection
from such vagaries.
The heartwood may not be seen again
until the tree falls.

≠

Getting Out

Pushing through the pain
You must go out
With each passing day
Urgency boils over
And yet, defying nature
You remain a caged beast
Pacing back and forth
When all the while
The door is open
But feelings prevail
And you prefer loneliness
Over unknown risks
Of a new world
It's a birth and it must happen
The contractions
Squeeze your world
Ever smaller in there
Filing at cage bars
Moving on to another
In despair about the first one
On some level
You know you are free
Longing for the comfort
The womb of your past
Holds you back
Mind and heart face off
You should
I can't
Then what now?
OK, I will

≠

Lost

I know these woods
I've been lost here before
Dense undergrowth
Swamps and briars

Look up to see where the sun is
It's cloudy
There are birds
They don't know where they're going
But they're OK being here

I could give up
Fall to the ground
I'd never be seen again
I swore I'd never do that

So on I plod
Look! A clearing!
No. Another swamp

After a while – like the birds –
I'll accept that I'm here
Only then is the path revealed
When I start looking here
Where I am now

Self-Denial

I push into my body
the defense of my weakness.
I can't. I need help. I need protection.
Subconscious thoughts
land at the base of my spine.
The root of my suffering.

The daily "have to", "don't want to" list
pits my own will against me.
Won't someone else
please do everything for me?
While I decay in idleness.
Where is my enabler?
My co-dependent rescuer?
What problem do I need to have
to compel your compassion?

When my dysfunction is so glaring,
even I can see it.
We're the last to know
what we won't admit.
We sneak it past ourselves
while we're unconscious.

Let me tell you what happened to me.
It's them!
They make me feel this way.
My world is unsafe now,
and I am weak.

A utopian mirage
keeps me seeking a way out
while the wound festers within.

Out and in
Now and then
Me and you
Where is the path to wholeness?

Dangling

It's the unfinished...
I thought that I...
Where are the...

Dangling.
Not knowing.
No logic.
No conclusion.

Always seeking.
Always wanting.
Always incomplete.

Train at the end of the tracks.
Disembark and wander
in the desert,
praying for rain.

The same dream
every night.
Wake up
before it's over.

The air is still.
The boat rests.
Crickets.

I keep thinking,
there must be something.
Why is it cloaked?
The past doesn't help.
It's already here.

Blinded by seeking.
Surrender.
Open your eyes.
Accept the gift,
as it is.

Reacting

"I can't handle this!"
Such dramatic throbbings
squawk from inside
like a smoke alarm
with no battery left.

I've learned to ignore it,
but on it goes,
predicting my demise.

I cannot count the times that I reacted
and thereby caused a fire;
each one just as easily put out
in a moment of clarity.

Now it vies pathetically
for my attention,
but I won't budge.
There will be no emergency today.

Largely invisible to others,
it can be inferred
like mosquitoes around a man
who swats at himself.
What else would explain this hiding?

It's in plain view
for those who also suffer it.
I used to avoid them -
afraid of catching their fire,
but let it burn!
It's only the ego.
The spirit is a phoenix.

≠

Part II: The Fog Lifts

When insight first dawns,
it feels victorious.
But it takes more than the mind
to get you off
of the rollercoaster.

Self Concept

We start eagerly as children,
building our selves
from whatever we find.
An unstable structure,
but we run with it.

Fragile self, standing alone,
seeks the mirror of others.
Tell me I'm real.
Tell me I matter.

There are cracks
and broken pieces,
and monsters under the bed.
But our whole life savings
is invested in this.

The cracks are filled
with uneasy busyness.
Monsters are sent to the dungeon.
A light wallpaper of optimism is plastered on.

It's all made of thoughts,
but it looks rather solid.
The others look solid too,
until the earth quakes beneath us.

Trying to patch it up,
though there is no foundation,
we put on an addition,
and a fancy edifice
that stands out in the community.

Then the first demon appears,
we anesthetize him.

The second demon appears.
We sleep though his visit.

The future keeps changing
and we wonder,
are we still in it?
The past also changes.
It looks different now.

The house shakes.
The dungeon door rattles,
and a jaguar stares
from the corner of my eye.

I turn and face him.
There is no defense.
Despair unlocks the dungeon.
All hell breaks loose.
I run from the house
before it falls.

Stumbling in shock.
Exposed and vulnerable.
Where am I?
Who am I?
Does anyone know?

The air is fresh
and the world is lovely,
but I frantically look for safety.

My call is answered.
The community responds.
A barn raising happens.

Now I stand on the threshold,
but I wonder,
is this me?

Lost Glory

There was a glory
whole and complete
as love without object.
Beyond any dazzling display of earth.

Growing human,
the inner eye closes.
We search a widening world

Pieces of splendor
Fragments of love
So promising
So fleeting
So painful
to see them go

Leaving us
grasping for another,
or trying to console
the lost child in us.
They cannot endure
because of the shelter
they require.

The pain,
flowing like lava,
breaches the walls.

In the full impact of loss,
disillusion opens the inner eye
for a moment.

*Enough for some
to lose interest
in their addiction
to the world.*

The Act

How did it start?

A little insight
balooned the ego
with hot air.
Pop! Down I came.

A little power
sparked the delusion -
I control things.
No. I don't.

Mind writes a script
and I perform.

I struggle
to stick to the script,
but the set changes.
Characters enter
Characters exit

At some point
I run out of lines.
At some point
I run out of props.

Is it over?
Intermission?
No, I'm still on stage!

It's improv now.
Suddenly aware of the audience -
witness of the play.

Turns out,
it was all for them,
and I thought it was me.

The Machine

Remember running wild?
Twirling, falling to the ground
Tree calling you skyward
Making up games
Stick becomes sword
En Garde!

It slowly turned serious
Winners and losers
That's against the rules
Time for dinner
Wash your hands
Bell rings
Next class
Report cards
Practice tonight
Driving lessons
What's your major
All-nighter
Paper's due
Fix the car
Interview
Dress right

Congratulations!
You got the job
The home
The marriage

But something went wrong
It's supposed to be great
You're supposed to be grateful

Stuck in a role
Mask on
Nobody sees you
Replaceable
One argument
One accident
One recession
And you're out
Mask off
Sign forms
Wait here
In this gown

Suddenly
You realize
I'm free!

Walk away
Wear whatever
Job is replaceable
Need less
Meditate
Look at stars
And wonder…

Being Human

I didn't want to come here.
I was pushed out of the womb.
Cast out of the garden.
A sweet longing to return
is a deeply buried seed,
that holds the memory of oneness.

The carnival of humanness
mesmerized me.
I was set apart
In a world of others.

My mind was trained
about endless distinctions.
The world was shattered
by words and concepts.

Still my heart rebelled
against the separation,
and thrust me into others
until they responded.

Life draws us out
again and again.

Short excursions
Waves on the beach
merely taste the sand
and then disappear.

Longer adventures -
the incoming tide.
Bathing in them I forget
that they too will leave me.

The joy of the world
is the serpent's call.
Tasting its sweetness
I think "At last, I've made it".
It leaves a hangover
when it's gone.

The ups and the downs
are part of the dance,
but I want off of the Ferris wheel.

It erodes me
and the seed is exposed.
A new wholeness takes root.

The carnival seems garish now.
I climb to the hub of the Ferris wheel
and the world spins around me.

The mind proposes another journey,
but the heart knows better.
Entering the silence,
I am the peace
that I've been seeking.

Existential Problem

I found out the other day
that I don't exist.
Someone finally told me.
Imagine how upset I was.

The paperwork is all there.
My family thinks I'm real,
but I have to admit
I was getting concerned
as pieces began falling out.

Too scared to look inside.
What if it's empty?
They say there's vast space
between the atoms,
but there are atoms, right?

I **did** exist once,
I think.
Then the past disappeared.
I keep assuming myself
into existence.
It works,
as long as no one checks.

An astute observer
called me out though.
Now that I know,
there's no point in pretending.
So now I've been looking
for what remains.

≈

The Myth of Separateness

Are we still living
as the myth of separateness?
Islands of awareness
We think it's inside of us,
spilling out in words.
As if the noise of our mouth
could bridge the waters.
We are more like the ocean
in which islands swim.
We only notice
when the borders grow thin
and permeable.
Some of me
washes up on your shore.
When time falls apart
and it all shows up now.
Even then,
we don't surrender.
We make something up,
and keep pretending
to be the trunk
of the elephant in the room.
But we are not parts
of anything.
We are singular.

From the Future

This is a message
that **YOU** sent from the future.

You won't believe what happened.
It's not your fault.
You did your best,
but nothing can prepare you.

There were little foreshadowings.
But even if you had noticed,
you would have dismissed them.

Maybe it's better
to not see it coming -
to live happily
in the fantasy
that things won't change.

But who could be that innocent?
Wouldn't anxiety sabotage you?
How long can life sail smoothly along
with no hurricane?

Maybe I shouldn't be telling you this.
Disregard what I said.
Just be ready for anything
and have a nice day

≈

Spoiler Alert

This is a message that **YOU** sent from the future.

You won't **believe** what happened!
It's really not a problem.
It's just amazing!

You played your role in it perfectly.
You could have seen it coming.
There were hints about it.
But even if you had noticed them
you still wouldn't have believed it.

Maybe it's even better
to not see it coming.
Just living your mundane life
and then **BAM!**

I'd love to tell you about it,
but maybe I shouldn't spoil it for you.
Disregard what I said.
Just be ready to be surprised
and have a nice day.

Enigma

Did you ever try
to explain your way
out of existence?
Only to find your words
rebuilding you?

Sliding under the voice
of the narrator in your head,
another voice appears.
Russian nesting dolls,
each with another inside.

Watching yourself watch your self,
like some mind-blowing
M. C. Escher print.
Pay no attention
to that man behind the curtain.

It's a trick you have played on yourself.
Trying to think your way out
pulls you farther into the quicksand.

The only way out is to drop it.
Stop winding the toy.
Wait quietly.
Ahhh. Here I am.

≈

The "G" Word

If we could, we'd like to talk about it,
or better yet
write it down in a book.
We can't, but we don't know that.
It would have to contain
all books and all authors within it.

Frustrated,
we fashion special symbols for it,
and talk about them
like they were things.

It's not like other nouns though.
If I say "tree",
one may see pine, another maple,
but there would still be roots;
there would be trunk and branches.

If I say this special syllable,
there would be unique thoughts and images
flashing through every mind.
And the differences matter to some.
Wars have been fought over this;
family and friends estranged.
Ironic, given that it is in fact
what makes one whole
out of all of us.

Ignorance argues over petty things.
Wisdom is silent.
Words get in the way.

≈

Why the Stories?

She wants to tell me
what she learned from her experience.
She is older and grayer for it.
There is wisdom in her story,
and she lights up
at the opportunity to tell it.
But it's the fifth time she has told me.

She doesn't have dementia.
She must know that she's
told this story before.
Impatience rises inside me.
"Yah, you told me that" I say,
but she goes on.
She just speeds up a little
so she can get it out
before I lose patience.

I remember when I was little
Grandma would read stories to me.
She was the only one
who could take my father's chair.
With me on her lap,
her wrinkled hand reached
for the same very old book,
and I always wanted her
to read the same stories
every time.

I used to think
that I don't tell the same stories
over and over,
until someone pointed out that I do.

I just don't say them out loud,
or to anyone else.

But my mind is a player piano.
The same damn stories
are stuck on shuffle play.
Some are in the past.
Others are in the future.
Some of them are lovely.
Some are horrendous.
All of them about me.

Why the endless repetition?
If the stories end,
the whole house of cards falls.
I have no idea who I am.
But of course,
I am.

I Don't Know

In the morning
the fog blankets me.
Unwilling to be myself
Unable to see beyond

Meditation, yoga, and black coffee
bring me around
then mercifully some light appears.

A master's words
spoken by a bird or a breeze
remind me
that I have made a problem of myself.

I laugh at my foolishness
and then it resumes.
I am partly cloudy today.
The best I can say of myself
is that I know when I don't know,
and it will pass.

I Made Up My Mind

I made up my mind
at the lumber yard.
Got materials and tools
and built it.

I made up my mind
at the grocery store.
Got the ingredients
and cooked it up.

I made up my mind
at the art supply store.
Got paint and canvas
and out-pictured it.

I made up my mind
at my parents' house
as a little kid.
A game of make believe.

I changed my mind.

About Time

Let's talk about time.
How long do you have?
A minute? An hour? 90 years?
It took decades for you to become this.

Does it vanish when you die?
The body does,
but that's not you.
You go on to infinity.

Are you stuck
being this same person forever?
Oh God no!
The universe is much kinder than that.

The problem is
that time destroys everything,
and that's also a gift.
Thankfully, you are not a thing.
You're a being.
There's a difference.

Things come into and out of existence
all the time.
They do that just for you.
Without an observer
nothing happens.
Just unmanifest possibilities.

But let's get to the point.
What are you up to
with that everlasting consciousness
that you are?

≈

B Movie

Reality as we know it
is a B movie.
Flimsy plot
Odd characters
The set doesn't even match the story

We should be laughing at it
but we take it seriously;
scream at the scary parts
and identify with the characters.

We don't even notice
that time is out of sequence
and parts of the set are missing.

Most people don't snap out of it
until it's over
and the credits start rolling.
They call that a life review.

It's a shame they weren't present
when it was happening.
A quick trip to the projection room
would have made it clear:
There's nothing out there.
It's all in here.

What Remains

I was a beast of burden;
Carrot dangling in front of me;
A crack of the whip behind.
Then I remembered
seeing through this façade once.

Retreating from life,
I climbed the mountain alone.
For a moment
the heavens opened up.
The stars told me
I am infinite.

A swarm of mosquitoes
waited at the base.
Housework neglected,
downtrodden again
but I knew there is more.

I sought out the others
who also knew.
Excited to talk with them,
we vowed to keep this alive.

We returned to work,
paid our bills,
complained about the news.

Talk turned to practice
and moved in with us.
First one, then another, then another.
Each worked for a while.
I kept riding this train,
hoping to arrive.

Life became ominous.
My practice wasn't enough.
It all fell apart.

I rebuilt it
but a great fear lurks inside.
If it fell before,
it will fall again.

A practice requires a student.
Students come and go.
Practice makes practice.
This train never arrives.
All things come and go.

***We** come and go.*
One thing remains:
awareness itself.

The Bridge to Nowhere

Expanding to burst the thought balloon.
Offering up existence to emptiness.
Not used up.
The ride continues, heart in throat
till I meet my beginning.

Self jumps out of the mirror
to finish me.
"A little longer" I say
but the heat is turned up
to the melting point.

"Why do I go on?" I wonder,
prolonging my stay
on the bridge to nowhere.
There's nothing but fog here...
...and me.

It's the fear of the void –
of nonexistence.
An imaginary abyss
created by fear.
Made of antimatter.
It vanishes upon contact with reality.
I'm dreaming right now,
and pressing snooze unconsciously.

≈

The Essence

Peeling off outer layers.
Ripping off Velcro attachments.
A process of elimination.
The customary uniform
of public persona.
The body itself
can be taken away,
without loss of essence.
Still more to go.
Dark energy to burn off.
The black hole
at the center of our galaxy
exerts its tug.
But this one escapes.
Not made of matter.
Untouched by time.
It cannot be known.
Why do I go on this way,
as if I could say something about it?

Searchlights Turned Inward

Before the story began,
shining out from behind
earliest memories
shafts of sun
piercing clouds,
there it is!

Wordforms mold and shape
riverbed of experience
winding and twisting
until the source disappears
from view.

An island cut off
from the motherland
no longer flowing free
confined to artificial borders
assumed to be real.

The monkey
climbs every tree
examines every rock and twig.
There must be more.

Standing up now
tall and proud
with sophisticated tools
I need more, ever more.

A swarm of thoughts
looks outside for answers
and finds only questions.

Flies buzz around me
exhausted

there is no place
to rest my head
among these questions.

One question
stamps out all others
"Who am I?".
This one does not accept words
as an answer.
It quietly erodes boundaries:
Inner and outer
Past and future
Me and you

Thoughts assert their priority.
Boundaries return.
Constricted again.
Who am I?
Rummage through memories.
A million answers come to mind.
None are convincing.

Trying to surrender
but this "I" is addictive.
Still thinks it can
make up an answer.

When searchlights turn inward
the words flee.
The subject evades the inquiry.

Who is thinking these thoughts?
Who watches them?
Will that one please come forward.

The Circus

In the morning.
Eyes unshuttered.
The game resumes.
Get in your vehicle.
Move your character.

All engrossing stream of consciousness
rushing around you.

Delicious and painful.
Beautiful and depressing.
Noble and cruel.

A circus sideshow.
We're all admitted
and linger for a while.

The time comes to dismiss it,
but the show must go on.
The clown winks at you.
You get the joke,
and begin to laugh.

A hole opens up
in the circus tent.
A shaft of light enters.

The circus will leave town.
You will watch it go.
It's meant to be exciting.
It's meant to be challenging.
You chose to have problems.

Now you hear the silence
of the noisy parade.
Now you see the emptiness
of the crowded scene,
and the being of the human,
even while doing.

December

As we run out of days
snow spreads a white sheet
over the death of autumn -
a bright white canvas
for life's renewal.

There will be a long pause
as the sun goes south.
The earth will try to brush us off.
We hide in our homes
and in our work.

In these days
we make our own light,
or languish in darkness.
But we are not extinguished,
and the sun is a little early every morning.

This is the time
when beings of light
make their appeal.

Awake from your dream,
for the world is lit
not merely by sunlight.
You too must also shine.

Part III: Illumination

When you step outside
of your own drama,
it loses its heaviness.
Now the light breaks through,
and enters your heart.

A Glimpse

There comes a time
when the ponderous burden
of being you
gives way.

When the dullness
of unwanted moments
cracks open
and a stunning silence appears.

In the emptiness of your mind,
the glory of being blossoms.

A moment of timelessness.
Every detail
inexplicably perfect.
Nothing is insignificant.
Clarity erases all boundaries
that thought invented.

You have been chosen
to be the witness
of this private miracle.
No one else could see it.

Even you
will think it nothing
when the freight train of thought
rumbles back in.

But each time it happens
the door opens a little wider.
One day you will remain.

∞

Where Words Can't Go

I am where words can't go.
Behind the eyes,
deep in the heart,
with a gaze so real and loving,
fear doesn't stand a chance.

I shine
with a light that goes through walls,
and makes the atoms dance inside you.
A fountain of peace
flowing out of me.

I am transparent and subtle.
An ethereal presence
which lifts you up
and reminds you
that this is who you are.

∞

The Real Firewalk

There are people who walk on fire.
Red hot coals
Bare feet
Mind over matter is the lesson.
It makes the mind bold and sharp
but who holds that sword?
Will it be beaten into plowshares?
Or used for personal gain?

There is another power.
Sublime,
it has no opponent.
While struggling to meet their needs,
most people miss it.

Some seek it as a solution
to their personal problems,
and lose faith
when problems return.

Others begin to sense it
when life is utterly unbearable.
Surrender and despair are the only options.
Some choose despair and are lost.

A few choose surrender;
then begins the real firewalk.
It begins with the hope
of personal salvation, restoration.
A vision of life repaired.
It's a mirage
but it makes you walk into the desert,
leaving behind many things.

Next tears of lava
come burning out of you.
Until you cross this river of lava
despair remains an option.

The eruptions subside.
There is emptiness
and the promise of peace.
But there is that lava.
Red hot,
and you know that's the path
but you doubt and hesitate.
Anything you try to take with you
will be burned to ashes.
You wonder what's left of you
and what could be on the other side.

You step into the lava
and then you realize
it is everything that you feared
and it's on fire!
You were afraid of your self
and it's on fire!

You never reach the other side.
Just as you are burned up,
you wake up.
You realize
that this whole drama
occurred in a mind
that thought it was separate,
that thought it was an object,
made of atoms,
that thought it could die,
that struggled to control things.

Now the personal nightmare ends.
A peaceful, humble person is there,
and you remain -
an immortal loving presence.

∞

What You Get

The world gives you back
whatever you bring to it.

Show up empty handed
and the world gives you nothing.

Bring your fear to it
and the world becomes frightening.

Bring anger
and the world attacks you.

Bring resentment
and the world becomes irritating.

Bring peace
and the world becomes comforting.

Bring appreciation
and the world becomes beautiful.

Bring unconditional love
and the world becomes heaven.

∞

Enlightenment

You live in the temple
that you were born in --
never been outside.

You look out the windows.
The glass is stained and dirty.
You grew up with those colors and splotches
imposed on the world.
You never knew of a world without them.

'Till someone told you
to scrub them until they're clear.
But where to scrub?
How long will it take?
You tire of scrubbing.

More dirt accumulates
until someone comes again
and opens the door.
Come out and see
where you've been.

It's revealed in an instant.
You're so happy
to stand in the sun
and scrub from the outside
where the dirt is obvious.

∞

The Truth

What is eternally real and true?

Oh mind,
receiving the answer would destroy you.
Do you still want to know?

Yes, for I am weary
from peace that turns to fear
and love that turns to sorrow.
I have become my own problem
and I cannot solve it.

You have read and heard many things.
Instead of freedom, they gave you belief.
Instead of reality, they gave you concepts.
Carrying this burden, you cannot enter.
Not knowing opens the door.

Anything you can think is not the truth.
I am the truth.

Your plan to find peace and happiness
blinds you to the ocean of these
that you drift upon.

Memories are a slow growing vine
that will strangle you
when its fruit is gone.

You chase after passing things
while eternity awaits you.
The eternal is only present now.
This is your opportunity
right now!

The body with its boundaries,
the mind with thoughts of separation,
are too confining for you.
Ignore the drama of life.
In the light of your presence
it is insignificant.

You stand on the diving board.
The eternal flame of presence
is now ignited.
There is no fear.
There is no sorrow.
Dive into this undefined moment.
Burn brightly as this presence.

∞

Windup Toy

My mind is troubled.
Good.

Negative thoughts,
even the body is upset.
I can't stand it!
Very good!

I have to do something about this.
Careful.

I remember what worked once.
You went to sleep.

Then what do I do about this?
Watch it, and let it be.

But I can't stand it!
Who can't stand it?

Me!
Then drop this "me".

How?
Lose interest in it.
It's not important.

It feels important to me.
It's a windup toy
that you think is your self.
Stop winding it.
You will awaken
when it becomes silent.

∞

The Ocean of Being

If you are alive,
something is working.
In this moment,
someone is born,
someone dies.

Life is not threatened by the future,
nor does it strain to be what it's not.
In this there is peace.

When I drop my story of you,
and you drop your story of me,
the foundation of harmony is laid.

Delighting in others,
requiring nothing of them,
opens the spigot of joy.

See the Self in everyone.
Dive into the ocean of being.

∞

Mass Awakening

For many painful centuries
we found no relief.
Barbaric power struggles.
The rule of tyrants' barren hearts;
devoid of empathy.
Civilization - a misnomer.

Democracy arrived with much fanfare
and bore a child that betrayed it.
The rule of money
sucked the life out of some
for the opulence of others.

Science brought new dominion,
undreamed of powers.
At the controls -
human minds, corporations and governments
full of insights and delusions,
kindness and hatred,
built the Internet and nuclear weapons.

The great acceleration of life
racing toward physical limits:
from sailing to space travel;
quill pens to live video.
Amplifies thoughts
and hastens manifestation.

The world shrinks.
Humanity swells.
There's no getting away
from each other now.

Rigid ideologies
make humans inhumane.
Hardliners draw steel lines in the sand,
turning "we the people" into "us and them".

Both sides descend into anger and fear.
Delusion makes killing others a solution.
The news spreads like wildfire.
In a world of bodies, borders, and bullets,
what could be more important?

But why is this man smiling?
And why is she so peaceful?
Are they out of their minds?
Don't they know what's happening?

Take a breath...
...pause and look again.

There's a unifying field
on a wavelength above and beyond thought;
a growing awareness.
Self-organizing, transpersonal awareness
takes over when we surrender.
It's been here all along,
unnoticed.

Consciousness itself
blossoms alongside of materialism.
It used to be rare.
Isolated avatars;
not understood.
Now little cells are popping up everywhere.

Even as the storm clouds
of self-destruction blacken the skies,

the great awakening throws a preemptive strike,
opening the doors of hearts and minds
to the light of day.

We abandon our old selves
which brought us no joy
and dwell in peace and love
regardless of what happens.

Now we say:
"I thought I was just one struggling human,
and then – OH. MY. GOD!
This is what religions were trying to tell us,
but we couldn't hear through our thoughts."

It dawns on us
that we are not things.
Not even stuck in a body.
Bodies are the experience
of the one spirit.

The powers that be dismiss us;
naïve and insignificant.
Our innocence belies the power that guides us.
Conscripting legions
through love and joy
until few indeed would hold a weapon,
and fewer still would fire it.

Deep down we wanted to stop the madness
but we were afraid of what would happen.
Around the world
growing numbers simply refuse
to be out of integrity.

So many tasks left undone.
Corporate, military, and government powers
stammer and stumble.
Widespread outages and shutdowns.
The dependent ones panic.

It's messy business
when the caterpillar is in the chrysalis.
Old body disassembled.
New one being built.

After a challenging adjustment,
the new order is established,
on earth as it is in consciousness.
Humans look on in awe
as a higher power makes a miracle
out of us in every moment.

We hold this truth to be self-evident:
that we are one consciousness
expressing in many forms,
and it is good.

∞

The Power

Waves of power
throb and pulse through the earth.
Something vast and primal
coursing through her veins.

The earth is basking
in the universal love
that galaxies are made of.

When I open that valve
in my heart,
it blows me away.

The throng of humanity rides it,
desperately trying to steer.

If my mind gets ahold of it
my own madness
builds a nightmare
and unleashes it.

I respect its sacredness.
I put myself at its disposal
and let go.

What appears chaotic
is a higher order.

Magnificent instrument that I am,
I belong
in the master's hands.

∞

The Fall from Grace: The Beginning

All things were one.
The Self was aware
of its unending bliss.
Time didn't exist, nor space.
Its infinite potential
was unmanifest.

It happened instantly.
The great vibrating existence
is the dream of God.
The idea of separate things
and separate times
with God's own awareness
pervading all of it.
It was perfect
and God knew it.

The glistening sweet harmony of it
was joined into one whole
by the one Consciousness.
This was the garden
where we entered the world.

∞

The Fall from Grace: The Fall

What a sweet time in the garden!
All dreaming God's exquisite dream.
Then the people started having their own ideas.
Looked harmless,
but they were cut off from God's one dream.
God let them go
knowing they'd be back.

Off we went to make our own lives
on this planet.
Finite little gods, living in time
and making it up as we went along.
Then one by one
we became trapped
in our own thinking.

There were beautiful thoughts
that made wondrous experience.
There were dark thoughts
that drew people in
deeper and deeper.
Then people started believing them.

And so what are you?
A dream within a dream
believing it's real.

∞

The Fall from Grace: The Hazards

It's a daring adventure
building your own life
with finite tools and no experience.
When your parents - and others - help you,
their mistakes become yours.
We acquire them as children -
congenital darkness.

The root of all suffering
The original sin
is believing you are separate.
It goes downhill from there.

Whatever we build on that foundation
will be unstable.
Although it will fall away one day,
while it's still standing
there are a few hazards
that deserve your attention.

∞

The Fall from Grace: Human Love

Pure Love has the power
to break through walls.
Light floods your heart and overflows.
Surrender to this,
but beware of the dark side of human love.

The infected mind feels a deep longing -
wanting love, lacking love.
It seeks fulfillment
as something to get from another.
True love flows naturally out of you.

When false love fails to satisfy,
or is thwarted altogether
you may descend into deeper darkness.
Feeling cut off from what you need
you blame others and manipulate.

At the bottom of this pit
you see only objects
where once there were people.
You treat them accordingly,
not seeing the harm
you do to yourself.

∞

The Fall from Grace: Needing More

Let the collective intelligence
conduct this symphony.
Enjoy the perfect harmony
as you watch the right action
performed through you.
You will never lack anything
required by this moment.

In your dream of separateness
it is all up to you.
If the only tool you have is a mind,
then everything looks like a problem.

The mind promises to solve it
but first you need a few things:
You need credentials.
You need money,
and most of all, you need time.

With enough of these you will be ok,
or so you think.
Goals are reached.
You have enough,
but you're not ok.

Now here is the trap:
You believe your mind
when it tells you
that you just need more.

∞

The Fall from Grace: The Body

The human form is a splendid instrument
through which the world's great performances are given.
Care for yours like a Stradivarius.
Keep it tuned up
and follow the conductor.
But know the difference
between the instrument
and the artist.

The body is finite.
You are not.
A piece of infinity
is still infinite.

A simple thought:
"I am this body"
makes so much fear.
Now it's a life and death struggle.
Life becomes heavy.
When the body is threatened
you are cast into darkness.
In the depth of this desperation
Hideous things can be justified.
All from one delusion --
"I am this body".

∞

The Fall from Grace: Memories

Memories are your vapor trail
streaking across the sky.
Man-made works of ephemeral beauty.
They may add layers of appreciation
on your experience.

In the mind's grasping hands,
formed and reformed,
each finds its place
in the story of you.

This is our street...before the tornado.
This is my Mom...I still miss her.
This is me...before the accident.

Replaying in slow-mo
reopen the wound
a ritual scarring
deep in neural pathways.

The failure
The loss
The embarrassment
Let them go.

And yet some,
sweet as honey,
echo the joy you once knew.

Grasping a rose
you recoil from the thorns.
But these treasured blooms
have thorns unnoticed
until buried deep.

The door is unlocked.
They steal your attention.
Staring in the rear-view mirror
as you careen ahead.

They send you down dead end roads
in futile attempts to recreate
what never really was
as you remember it.

Let each snowflake be unique,
and melt on your tongue
in child-like delight.
Stay here,
where something else
you never dreamed of
is possible.

∞

The Fall from Grace: The Mind

The mind is man's ultimate machine.
Programmed and sent to boot camp.
Disciplined until it falls in line
with millions of others;
a monster of such complexity and scale
it can scarcely be managed.
Bingeing on resources
and throwing up buildings and roads
all over the place.

You were already strapped into the cockpit
before the age of reason.
Perhaps you resented those straps.
The power and control are seductive
but it costs your freedom.

Like countless ones before you,
you gorged yourself
on knowledge, theories, and stories –
being right and in control.
The whole world was stuffed
inside your head until it hurt.

This is a suffering
that many bear unknowingly.
Unless you've been outside,
the mind is irrefutably
the only perspective.
The great machine rolls on
in the name of progress,
often crushing what is in the way.

Too complex to be stable,
under extreme pressure

your mind crashes.
Everyone has their limit.
While still depending on it,
you press the eject button.

Being, without thinking,
once a vague idea,
is pressed into service
in such emergencies.

A traitor to the mind,
you fall in love with Being.
The mind calls it nonsense.
The full power of the machine
that took you decades to build
turns against you.

It seems so real and menacing.
The tanks and helicopters
eventually run out of fuel
if you don't flinch.
The trick is
never let it refuel
by believing its terrible story
is important
because it's about you.
You are the host.
It wouldn't dare kill you.

Next your own voice
whispers grave existential threats
in your ear:
You'll be nobody.
You'll be nothing.
And it's true.

In your place
a serene presence
embraces all that is.

If the moment requires,
the mind will serve
and then subside
within the vast silence
of your being.

∞

The Fall from Grace: The Return

In the bluster of youth
we say "I've got this!",
and throw ourselves into life,
with expectations of mastery.

No one told us of hazards.
We would not have listened.
We danced into the mine field
and blew ourselves away.

It's sweet sometimes
but it's a house of cards
that we gamble on.
We are bound to fall.

Ensnared in the hazards.
A forced march
through the cruelty
of our own projections.

Putting it outside
leaves us alone and vulnerable.
Fear bars the door.

A condition so alien to the spirit
that it cannot abide it.
A voice cries out in the wilderness:
This is not who I am!

There is a seed of beatitude.
No matter how deep you buried it,
it sprouts in your darkest hour,
when nothing is working.
You look for the door.

It will push through manure
toward a light still unseen
which is waiting for you.
One by one
you discard any hindrance
to its unfolding.

A lotus stands in the muddy bottom,
reaches through murky waters.
Knowing its destiny,
it breaks through the surface
and opens to the sun.
Taking its place once again
in the garden,
with vastly deepened appreciation.

∞

Gratitude

No one created themselves.
No one is ever alone.
We each have many to thank
for who we have become.

A tribute to my wife:
October Clarke Craig
1946 – 2018

For Those Who Miss October

Ancestors with facility
in language and performance.
Strange thread of disability
binds the family tree.

Beloved first born child
in the city that never sleeps.
Her given name – October,
a secret that she keeps.

Their dream of sweet suburbia
a crucible of despair
when mother's crippling polio
left her isolated there.

It's living through adversity
that made their spirits fit.
The mother of invention
brought humor, will, and wit.

Hiding under blankets
with a flashlight and a book.
Reading was her first love,
and she was clearly hooked.

First attempt at marriage,
on the heels of Vietnam,
ends when he wants children,
but she'll be more than mom.

She makes her mark in publishing.
She sets her standards high.
Not one missing comma,
passed her attentive eye.

Her eloquence on occasion
festooned with baroque flourishes.
Blunt when necessary
but humor is what she cherishes.

She decided Boston
was on her freedom trail.
There she made a new start.
There she would set sail.

All the corporate bullshit
got her quite annoyed.
She put it all behind her.
Now she's self-employed.

While she was in Boston
she met a younger man.
They went on to marry,
though that was not his plan.

To say she had no children
isn't quite the truth,
for she was like a mother
to several in their youth.

Her frightening diagnosis
many didn't know.
It never did define her.
She never let it show.

Her nerves would fail her later,
oddly like her mom.

Her spirit just kept going -
surprisingly aplomb.

Teacher, leader, chaplain,
and editor of books.
A friend to the discouraged
no matter what it took.

She had a major presence.
It's where she would be known.
In church communities,
she gathered with her own.

It's more the way she listened
than words that showed she cared.
Her soft blue eyes would glisten
at someone's soul laid bare.

Anyone could feel it -
full of warmth and grace.
Generous attention
as she looked into your face.

It's this we should remember.
It's ours to carry on,
to honor dear October,
now that she is gone.

∫

Finding the Truth

Once upon a time,
there was no Internet.
No television.
No telephone.
No radio.
No car.
No train.
Very few books.
Copied by hand.

The rare person
with a passion for truth,
set out on a pilgrimage
for the revered place
where the master
was rumored to be.
Hoping to be granted an audience.

Then came presses and newspapers
and trains and libraries.
There you would find
what they thought fit to print,
and no more.
Work with that,
or off on pilgrimage again.

Then came radios and telephones
and cars and greater freedom
of speech and press.
Word got around more quickly now.
But it was common business
and entertainment,
with deeper insights rarely found.

*The discerning reader
finds a few treasured books
that point the way.*

*In forty years
the world went crazy.
Hyper-connected.
Search engine optimized.
Everyone can know anything.
The boundaries of cultures,
religions, even language,
starting to blur.
Censorship is becoming impossible.
The highest wisdom
is streaming to your phone,
or the most degrading trash.
Now it's up to us.*

∫

I Was Restored

When my peaceful demeanor
was in a torrent of drama,
how blessed am I
that family and friends showed faith in me.

Patient listening, persistent support,
calmed the troubled waters.
A level of assistance
quite unreasonable to ask for,
met each need as it occurred.

It is not a small thing
to visit a grieving friend.

A parade of professionals,
not mere uniforms of customary service,
but whole human beings
engaged heart and soul with mine.

Their service alone is a privilege.
Offering themselves as well
is above and beyond.

When I asked to awaken,
the teacher appeared.
Grace stripped away transient things,
and shed its light on my deepest fears.
Grace said to me:
Blessed are you.
You have peace.
You have love.
You have joy.
Now give them away, and they will grow.

∫

Thank You

Thank you for friends
wherever I may go.
Thank you for teachers
when I need to know.

Thank you for winking
with synchronicities.
Thank you for showing
what human eyes can't see.

Thank you for problems
that require me to grow.
Thank you for patience
when I'm moving rather slow.

Thank you for the miracle.
How all things came to be.
And thank you for the poems
that didn't come from me.

∫

About the author

Peter Craig has lived an outwardly unremarkable life. Grew up in the small town of Moosup, CT; graduated from the University of Connecticut; had a career in Software Engineering; married October Clarke; owned a home in southern New Hampshire.

The couple was much loved by their church community, family and friends, and had a significant impact in their personal relationships. They shared a deep commitment to their spiritual life. For about 10 years, Peter devoted himself to caring for October as she became progressively more disabled by Multiple Sclerosis.

October's death in 2018 was a painful loss for Peter, and that is reflected in the early part of this book. With the support of many, he went through the stages of recovery and beyond to renewal and awakening.

Peter has written poetry on and off since childhood. He had no formal training in poetry, and rarely shared it with others. Following October's death he resumed writing poetry and began sharing it at local poetry meetings and open mic events.

Subjectively, it is quite a remarkable experience to be awake in this moment. I sense the awakening of our oneness, which we have always been, but were largely unconscious of. It is my joy to play any role in this process.

If you want to contact me about this book, please send email with the word "illumination" in the subject to: books@octoberc.com.